OUR CHURCH COVENANT

An Explanation of the New Hampshire Covenant

Our Church Covenant: An Explanation of the New Hampshire Church Covenant

ISBN: 978-1-105-74805-9

Contents

Church Covenant

Having been led by the Holy Spirit to receive the Lord Jesus Christ as our Savior (John 3:6,16), and on the public confession of our faith (Heb. 10:22-23), having been baptized in the name of the Father, and of the Son, and of the Holy Spirit (Matt. 28:19-20), we do now, in the presence of God and this assembly, solemnly and joyfully enter covenant with one another, as an expression of the one body in Christ (Acts 2:46).

We purpose, therefore, by the aid of the Holy Spirit (Eph. 5:18), to walk together in Christian love (Eph. 5:2), to strive for the advancement of the Church in knowledge, holiness and peace (Col. 1:10; I Thess. 4:3; Eph. 4:3), to promote its prosperity and spirituality (Acts 2:47), to attend its services regularly (Heb. 10:24), to sustain its worship (I Tim. 2:1-2), ordinances (Matt. 28:19-20), discipline (II Thess. 3:14-15), and doctrine (Titus 2:1); to give it a sacred preeminence over all institutions of human origin (I Cor. 3:17), to give faithfully of time and talent in its activities (Eph. 5:16; I Pet. 4:10-11), to contribute cheerfully and regularity (II Cor. 9:7), as God has prospered us (I Cor. 16:2), to the support of the ministry (I Tim. 5:17-18), the relief of the poor (II Cor. 8:4), and the spread of the Gospel throughout all nations (I Cor. 9:4-7).

We also purpose to maintain family and private worship (Dan. 9:4-19), to train our children according to the Word of God (Deut. 6:4-9), to walk carefully in the world (Eph. 5:15; Col. 4:5), to be just in our dealings (I Pet. 2:12), faithful in our engagements (I Cor. 4:2), and exemplary in our conduct (I Cor. 11:1), to avoid all gossip (I Tim. 5:13), speaking that which is evil (I Pet. 2:12), and unrighteous anger (Eph. 4:31), to abstain from all forms of activity which dishonor our Lord Jesus Christ (I Cor. 10:31), cause stumbling to a fellow believer (I Cor. 8:9) or hinder the winning of a soul to Christ (I Cor. 10:27-28), to be zealous in our efforts to advance the cause of Christ, our Savior (II Cor. 5:20), and to give Him preeminence in all things (Col. 1:12-13).

We further purpose to encourage one another in the blessed hope of our Lord's return (I Thess. 4:13-5:11; Titus 2:13), to watch over one another in brotherly love (I Thess. 3:12), to remember each other in prayer (Jas. 5:14-18), to aid each other in sickness and distress (II Cor. 1:8-11), to cultivate Christian sympathy in feelings and courtesy in speech (Eph. 4:32,29), to be slow to take offense, (Jas.1: 19-20), but always ready for reconciliation (Col. 3:13).

We moreover purpose that when we remove from this place, we will as soon as possible unite with some other church of like faith and order where we can carry out the spirit of this covenant and the other principles of God's Word (Rom. 16:1-2). In the event there is no church, we shall seek, under the guidance of theSpirit's leading, to establish one (I Cor. 16:19).[1]

[1] This is the New Hampshire Covenant as found in J. Newton Brown's *Baptist Church Manual* (Philadelphia, 1853), 23, 24.

Introduction

Covenants are very common in our heritage as Americans. We have all heard of the Mayflower Compact, wherein our first Pilgrim Fathers entered into a mutual contract with one another, saying that they "solemnly and mutually, in the presence of God, and one another, covenant and combine ourselves together into a civil body politic."[2]

In the same vein, early Separatists in New England formed their entire culture around the idea of a mutual covenant before the Lord. In fact, the soul of New England is found in the way in which the society and church were connected via the covenant.3 This idea of a social contract continues to be the fabric of our society, and the backbone of our political structures. It is found everywhere in our lives: our constitution with its political structures, our economic with its financial forms, and our domestic lives with its marriage covenants.4 And it is especially found in the church and its life.[5]

Most churches with a congregational polity have a church covenant.[6] Congregationally run churches include Congregationalist churches, Baptist Churches, Bible Churches, and various types of other independent churches. This

---

[2] Since this document is everywhere to be found on the Internet, I will not seek to document it. While there are noted variations within the text, these textual variants have no bearing upon this issue.

[3] See Harry S. Stout, *The New England Soul: Preaching and Religious Culture in Colonial New England* (New York: Oxford University Press, 1986), pp. 21-23.

[4] See Larzer Ziff, "The Social Bond of Church Covenant," American Quarterly, 10 (1958), 454-62; Edmund Morgan, *The Puritan Family: Religion and Domestic Relations in Seventeenth-Century New England* (New York: Harper, 1966*);* James T. Johnson, "The Covenant Idea in the Puritan View of Marriage," *Journal of the History of Ideas,* 32 (1971:, 107-118.

[5] "It had been the self governing Greek republic, ruled by elected office-bearers; hereafter the communities of Christians, which were to be the ecclesiae, were to be little self-governing societies where the individual rights and responsibilities of the members would blend harmoniously with the common good of all," Thomas M. Lindsay, *The Church and the Ministry in the Early Centuries* (London: Hodder and Stoughton, 1903), p. 5.

[6] For a thorough discussion on the history of church covenants, see Champlin Burrage, *The Church Covenant Idea: Its Origin and Development* (Philadelphia: American Baptist Publication Society, 1904).

covenanting has been the practice for at least five centuries, and some data suggests that it has been the practice of independent churches since the apostolic era.

Our church has such a covenant. Every member is asked to enter into it upon admission into the church membership, and a copy of the covenant, which was signed by the original charter members, hangs on a wall in the basement of the church. To many the idea of entering the church covenant is some perfunctory act of ceremonial initiation. However, it is far from that.

I recently was asked about our covenant's significance. What is its role in the life of this church? Is that role something that is biblical? What are its purposes? How is it structured? How does it, or how should it, have a practical impact upon our church? These are surely legitimate questions, and it would do well for us consider them as a church for a moment. After all, it is something that every member is asked to agree with; and if something is worth entering into, it is should be worth commenting upon.

The Functional Significance of the Church Covenant

Well, let us begin with the basic question about the function of the covenant in the life of the church. Simply stated, the function of the church covenant is to highlight the necessity of having a regenerate membership. Fundamental to a Baptist church is the concept that a church is to receive none into its membership but such as evidence the new birth. It is here that we find the core significance of the covenant. It does this is in a number of ways, which I want to outline.

Constitution of the Church

First, when a church constitutes, a covenant is almost always implied, and the Baptist seeks to make this explicit. In many ways the church covenant is an idea that is both integral to the very nature of the church and basic to the essence of congregational life. Let me explain. *Let us begin with the very definition of the church.* What is a church? I think that any biblical definition of the church involves necessarily the idea of covenant. Speaking to this very thing, *The Cambridge Platform* puts the matter forth in a powerful manner:

> *This form being by mutual covenant, it followeth, it is not faith in the heart, nor the profession of that faith, nor cohabitation, nor baptism. 1. Not faith in the heart, because that is invisible. 2. Not a bare profession, because that declareth them no more to be members of one church than another. 3. Not cohabitation: atheists or infidels may dwell together with believers. 4. Not baptism, because it presupposeth a church estate, as circumcision in the Old Testament, which gave no being to the church, the church being before it, and in the wilderness without it. Seals presuppose a covenant already in being. One person is a complete subject of baptism, but one person is incapable of being a church.*[7]

For this reason, many have defined the church along these lines. For example, our own Confession of Faith, which is the New Hampshire Confession, the most widely used Calvinistic Baptist creed in America, states,

> *A New Testament church of the Lord Jesus Christ is a local body of baptized believers who are associated by covenant in the faith and fellowship of the gospel, observing the two ordinances of Christ, committed to His teachings, exercising the gifts, rights, and privileges invested in them by His Word, and seeking to extend His gospel to the ends of the earth.*[8]

Let us also consider the description of the church. The church is not merely individuals getting together.[9] Rather, it is an organism that has order. It is described as a body or a building. There is an organized union of the various parts. *The Cambridge*

---

[7] Williston Walker, *The Creeds and Platforms of Congregationalism* (New York: The Pilgrim Press, 207-208. Walker cites John Cotton, *The Way of the Churches* (New York: AMS Press, 1984), *pp. 2-4.*

[8] "That whereby the Church is as a *city compacted* together, is the Covenant," *John Davenport, Power of Congregational Churches Asserted and Vindicated* (London, 1672), p. 37; "Mutual covenanting and confederating of the Saints in the fellowship of the faith according to the order of the Gospel, is that which gives constitution and being to a visible Church," Thomas *Hooker, Survey of the Summe of Church Discipline* (New York, Arno Press, 1971), p. 46; "For the joyning of faithfull Christians into the fellowship and estate of a Church, we finde not in Scripture that God hath done it any other way then by entering all of them together (as one man) into an holy Covenant with himselfe."*John Cotton, The Way of the Churches."* p. 2.

[9] This phrase should not be taken to indicate the church is merely an organized group. It is something far more than this. It is the Body of the Risen Christ, possessed with spiritual life and spiritual gifts. "These various gifts are bestowed on different members of the Christian society for the edification of all, and they serve to show that it is one organism, where the whole exists for the parts, and each part for the whole and for all the other parts. They also show that the Christian society is not a merely natural organism; there is divine life and power within it, because it has the abiding presence of Christ; and the proof of His presence is the possession and use of these various 'gifts,' all of which come from the one Spirit of Christ in fulfillment of the promise that He will never leave nor forsake His Church. Their presence is a testimony to the presence of the Master which each Christian community can supply. It is a Church of Christ if His presence is manifested by these fruits of the Spirit which come from the exercise of the 'gifts,' which the Spirit has bestowed upon it; for the Church as well as the individual Christian is to be known by its fruits," Thomas Lindsay, *The Church and the Ministry,* 8-9.

Platform explains how these symbols of the church point to a covenant.

> *Saints by calling must have a visible political union among themselves, or else they are not yet a particular church, as those similitudes hold forth, which the scripture makes use of to show the nature of particular churches, as a body, a building, a house. Hands, eyes, feet, and other members must be united, or else (remaining separate) are not a body. Stones, timber, though squared, hewn and polished, are not a house, until they are compacted and united ; so saints or believers in judgment of charity, are not a church, unless orderly knit together.1 Cor. xii. 27. 1 Tim. iii. 15, Eph. ii. 22. 1 Cor. xii. 15, 16, 17. Rev. ii.*[10]
>
> *Particular churches cannot be distinguished one from another, but by their forms: Ephesus is not Smyrna, nor Pergamus, Thyatira, but each one a distinct society of itself, having officers of their own, which had not the charge of others ; virtues of their own, for which others are not praised; corruptions of their own, for which others are not blamed.*
>
> *This form is the visible covenant, agreement, or consent, whereby they give up themselves unto the Lord, to the observing of the ordinances of Christ together in the same society, which is usually called the church covenant: For we see not otherwise how members can have church power one over another mutually. The comparing of each particular church to a city, and unto a spouse, seemeth to conclude not only a form, but that that form is by way of covenant. The covenant, as it was that which made the family of Abraham, and children of Israel, to be a church and people unto God, so it is that which now makes the several societies of Gentile believers to be churches in these days (Exod, xix. 5, 8. Deut. xxix. 12, 13. Zech. xi.*

---

[10] Ibid., 207. This seems to be drawn from Richard Mather's *Aplogie for Church-Covenant (New York, Arno Press, 1972), p. 5*

14, and ix. 11. Eph. ii. 19. 2 Cor, xi. 2. Gen. xvii. 7. Deut. xxix. 12, 13. Eph. ii. 12, 18).

Now, if you will stop and think about this for a moment, you will see that this idea is very practical and full of common sense. The church's Confession of Faith, is not a set of one man's belief. It is the congregation's profession to the others. And when the congregation gathers together to constitute as a church, they are covenanting with one another in this single confession.

This covenanting may be either implicitly or explicitly done, but it is a matter of fact that is being done. Congregational polity recognizes this and seeks to be deliberate in this act. Explicit covenanting is the formal cause of a particular visible gospel church. John Owen explains,

> *Whereas, therefore, in the constitution of a church, believers do give themselves up unto the Lord, and are bound solemnly to engage themselves to do and observe all the things which Christ hath commanded to be done and observed in that state, whereupon he hath promised to be present with them and among them in an especial manner...their so doing hath the nature of a divine covenant included in it; which is the formal cause of their church-state and being.*[11]

Someone may say, "Yes, I see your point. But is that not what the Confession of Faith is all about?" Well, the Confession of Faith does have an important role in the forming of a church, but it not the only thing that has a role. The Confession is something that is a matter of doctrine, while the covenant is a matter of practice. One sets forth what a person must believe to be a member, the other sets forth what a person must do in order to be a member. The one establishes the required creed of the member, but the other establishes the required conduct of the member. In this, they work together. Leonard Woods, a noted

---

[11] John Owen, "The True Nature of a Gospel Church," in *The Works of John Owen,* edited b William Goold (London: Johnstone and Hunter, 1853), XVI:27. See the appendix with Owen's chapter entitled "Of the Formal Cause of a Particular Church."

Congregationalist of the 19th century, speaking on this in his *Report on Congregationalism*, states,

> *The instrument by which individual believers are constituted one body in a church, is a confession of faith in Christ and in the principles of his gospel, together with a covenant, wherein they mutually agree to give themselves up to the Lord, and unitedly to observe his ordinances.*[12]

When you come to an area and look for a church to join, you will normally seek those who are in agreement with you concerning the faith. So what do you do? You naturally look at their creed, the articles of faith, or Confession of Faith. What do they believe about Christ, the atonement, justification, the new birth, etc. They must be right there.

Let us say that they have a creed in which you can give your hearty consent. Is that all? I am sure that you and I have seen churches with fine statements of faith, but, upon arriving, we have not been as enthusiastic about the church. There were certain practices of the church that were bothersome to us. Therefore, if we are wise, we go to the church and see what it is all about.

There is a great lesson here. While the confession tells you that it is something worth looking at, there is something else that must be considered: the practice of the church. You want to see how they implement this creed into the daily life of the congregation. In reality, you are seeking to see whether or not the congregation that claims to be regenerate is acting regenerate. The covenant is designed to help the congregation live in a regenerate way.

Membership of the Church

Second, when admitting new members, the covenant idea is present. A church covenant should never be merely a document whose primary value comes from a one-time use in forming a

[12] Leonard Woods, *Report on Congregationalism: including a manual on church discipline* (Boston: Perkins and Company, 1846), 26.

church and then being placed in a cornerstone or hung upon a wall. Rather, the covenant should be seen as a living agreement whose biblical principles offer continuing sustenance for a church genuinely trying to be regenerate. Therefore, it is vitally important that newly admitted members also covenant with the rest of the church.

Immediately, the continuing, living value of the covenant comes into full sight. The covenant creates a sense of community among members of an individual congregation. As Governor Winthrop of early New England put it, "If a man enters no covenant, then is he not tied to one Church more than to another."[13] In other words, the church covenant forms the foundation of church relationships, assuming equality among the members of the congregation.

In addition to this equality of believers, it sets forth the brotherhood of members, reminding us that each member is a mutal child of God and, therefore, bound one to another for eternity! It gives flesh to unity, and it gives expression to the very idea of church unity. By it, we tangibly belong one to another. Again, *The Cambridge Platform* states,

> *All believers ought, as God giveth them opportunity thereunto, to endeavor to join themselves unto a particular church, and that in respect of the honor of Jesus Christ, in his example and institution, by the professed acknowledgment of, and subjection unto the order and ordinances of the gospel; as also in respect of their good of communion, founded upon their visible union, and contained in the promises of Christ's special presence in the church; whence they have fellowship with him, and in him one. with another; also, for the keeping of them in the way of God's commandments, and recovering of them in case of wandering, which all Christ's sheep are subject to in this life, being unable to return of themselves; together with the benefit of their mutual edification, and of their posterity, that they may not be cut*

[131313] John Winthrop, "Letter from John Winthrop to the Rev. Henry Painter (1635), in Winthrop, *Life and Letters of John Winthrop* (Boston: Little, Brown and Company, 1869), 2:416-17.

off from the privileges of the covenant. Otherwise, if a believer offends he remains destitute of the remedy provided in that behalf. And should all believers neglect this duty of joining all particular congregations, it might follow thereupon, that Christ should have no visible political churches upon earth. Acts ii. 47, and ix. 26. Matt. iii. 13, 14, 15, and xxviii. 19, 20. Psalms, cxxxiii. 2, 3, and Ixxxvii. 7. Matt, xviii. 20. 1 John, i. 3. Psalms, cxix. 176. 1 Peter, ii! 25. Eph. iv. 16. John, xxii 24, 25. Matt, xviii. 15, 16, 17.[14]

Commitment to the Church

Third, when relating daily with one another, the covenant becomes significant. Voluntary commitment to the contents of the covenant adds to its value in church life. A person becomes a church member by choice, not by force. But once he becomes a member, he is expected to participate in the life of the church. In short, it minimizes the possibility of a merely nominal attachment to the Christian community.

The biblical obligations, voluntarily accepted in becoming a member of a Baptist church, require covenantal embodiment and fulfillment in the total affairs of life. A healthy view of the covenant stresses the ethics of church membership. Each member is called upon to try extremely hard to conform daily to the demands delineated in the covenant about our mutual relationships.

Perhaps the most important value of the covenant is its role in constantly reminding church members of the moral and spiritual duties and privileges to which they had initially committed themselves in uniting with the church. A covenant worth having is a covenant worth living; and a covenant worth entering into is a covenant worth being obligated to keep. Speaking directly to the "Individual Responsibility of Church Members" in relationship to the church covenant, the 1846 circular letter of the Meredith Baptist Association in New Hampshire states,

---

[14] Walker, *The Creeds and Platforms of Congregationalism*, 209.

The religion of Jesus Christ is consistent in all its parts. There is no disagreement between the principles it inculcates and the practice it requires. Primitive saints first gave themselves to the Lord, and then unto one another by the will of God. Responsibility was shared alike. So, brethren, when you gave yourselves to the Lord it was in a covenant never to be broken. Such was your sense of responsibility, that, without any reserve, you consecrated your all to God — your time, your talents, your property, your intellectual powers, and all your moral influence. The vows you then took upon you, you assumed deliberately, freely and cheerfully, while a cloud of witnesses compassed you about. The world, saints, angels, God, gazed on you, while you dedicated yourselves, to Christ and the church. Brethren, can you ever forget those solemn vows? When you joined yourselves unto the Lord, and unto his people by the will of God, did you divide your responsibilities among those with whom you connected yourselves in church fellowship, so as, in fact, to diminish your previous personal obligation? Far otherwise; the moment you crossed the threshold of the church your responsibilities were greatly increased; they sprung out of your new relation; they were imposed by your new privileges. From that memorable hour you have been bound to make the glory of God and the salvation of the world the constant aim and effort of your life, according to your opportunities and the measures of your moral capacities; and this obligation will ever remain unalterably the same; it will be recognized and acted on in the decisions of the Last Day.[15]

In our day, we see even Christians taking too lightly their contractual commitment –whether it is in their marriages, mortgages, or memberships. This sadly resembles the words of the Apostle Paul about the last days, when he says that men are

---

[15] *Minutes*, Meredith Baptist Association (New Hampshire), 1846, 13. Quoted in Charles W. Deweese, *Baptist Church Covenants* (Nashville, Broadman Press, 1990), x –xi.

trucebreakers.[16] As Christians, we should be like our Lord, who is faithful to all His covenant engagements. I am thankful that the habit of the people within this congregation is faithfulness to the covenant. I do not believe that is done merely because it is an obligation, but it is a loving expression to both the Lord and His people.

[16] 2 Timothy 3:3. 'It properly means "without treaty;" that is, those who are averse to any treaty or compact. It may thus refer to those who are unwilling to enter into any agreement; that is, either those who are unwilling to be reconciled to others when there is a variance - implacable; or those who disregard treaties or agreements. In either case, this marks a very corrupt condition of society. Nothing would be more indicative of the lowest state of degradation, than that in which all compacts and agreements were utterly disregarded'-- Albert Barnes.

The Biblical Ground for the Church Covenant

Now, it is important that we address the biblical grounds for a church covenant. Congregational churches have historically set out to pattern their churches after the biblical pattern of the New Testament, thought they have not always been successful. When it comes to the church covenant, we must ask, "Have they followed a biblical pattern, or have they invented something?" Obviously, this is not a small issue, seeing that we must be regulated by the Word of God alone. In addition to the statements made above, let me provide the following arguments that seem to support the view that church covenants are indeed biblical.

Structure of Biblical Revelation

First, we can say clearly that the entire structure of God working with men is solidly based on a covenant. In fact, we divide the entire Bible into two main sections –the Old Testament and the New Testament. God has forever united us to Himself and us to others by the means of covenants. No one can understand the Bible without understanding the idea that God relates to man through covenants. As Eugene Merrill has stated, the idea of the covenant is "the key to a proper biblical hermeneutic and theology is to be found in the covenant concept of both the OT and NT."[17]

Structure of Secular Relations

Secondly, we also see mutual covenants concerning secular things. We see it in the lives of Abraham and Isaac when they made a covenant with Abimelech over the wells of water (Gen. 21:27; 26:29). Jacob also made a covenant with Laban, when Jacob set up pillars of a witness of the covenant (Gen. 31:45f.). Other covenants are found throughout the entire Word of God.

---

[17] Eugene H. Merrill, "Covenant and The Kingdom: Genesis 1-3 as Foundation for Biblical Theology," *Criswell Theological Review* 12 (1987) 295-308.

Others include Jonathan and David in 1 Sam. 18:3, 4; 20:16; 2 Sam. 21:7 and Ahab with Ben Hadad in 1 Kings 20:34;.

God warned Israel repeatedly not to covenant with non-Israelites (Ex. 23:32; 34:12; Deut. 7:2; Judges 2:2), and He required that they keep any vows that they did make, as in the case with the Gibeonites who tricked them (Josh. 9:19; see also the punishment of another breached man-with-man covenants in 2Sa 21:1-6; Je 34:8-22; Ezek. 17:13-19). The idea of secular covenants is even found today in our daily businesses and our marriages. Covenants have been part of the fabric of social life since the dawn of humanity, and they are not to be easily broken.

Structure of Informal Religious Associations

Third, men have entered voluntarily into a religious covenant with one another to seek God. For example, we find Asa making a covenant with the people of Judah and Benjamin. They had heard the message of the Lord by the means of Oded the Prophet, who said, "The LORD is with you, while ye be with him; and if ye seek him, he will be found of you; but if ye forsake him, he will forsake you" (2 Chronicles 15:2). They responded by repenting of their sins and seeking the Lord. This is the record we have in verses 12 through 15:

> *And they entered into a covenant to seek the LORD God of their fathers with all their heart and with all their soul; That whosoever would not seek the LORD God of Israel should be put to death, whether small or great, whether man or woman. And they sware unto the LORD with a loud voice, and with shouting, and with trumpets, and with cornets. And all Judah rejoiced at the oath: for they had sworn with all their heart, and sought him with their whole desire; and he was found of them: and the LORD gave them rest round about. (2 Chronicles 15:12-15)*

The covenant consisted of two parts: 1. We will seek the God of our fathers with all our heart, and with all our soul. 2. Whosoever, great or small, man or woman, will not worship the true God, and serve him alone, shall be put to death. Thus no toleration was given to idolatry, so that it must be rooted out: and that this covenant might be properly binding, they confirmed it with an oath; and God accepted them and their services.

Another example is found in Nehemiah 9. This time it is found when the returning children of Israel are lamenting over their sin and failure to obey the Lord. Almost the entire 9th chapter is a prayer of confession. As we come to the end of it we read, "And because of all this we make a sure covenant, and write it; and our princes, Levites, and priests, seal unto it" (Nehemiah 9:38). This written document was designed to express their heart's desire, to restrain their backslidings, and to stir them to duty by being a witness against them if in the future they were unfaithful to their engagements. Discussing this, Matthew Henry writes,

> *Here is the result and conclusion of this whole matter. After this long remonstrance of their case was made they came at last to this resolution, that they would return to God and to their duty, and oblige themselves never to forsake God, but always to continue in their duty. "Because of all this, we make a sure covenant with God; in consideration of our frequent departures from God, we will now more firmly than ever bind ourselves to him. Because we have smarted so much for sin, we will now stedfastly resolve against it, that we may not any more withdraw the shoulder." Observe, 1. This covenant was made with serious consideration. It is the result of a chain of suitable thoughts, and so is a reasonable service. 2. With great solemnity. It was written, in perpetuam rei memoriam - that it might remain a memorial for all ages; it was sealed and left upon record, that it might be a witness against them if they dealt deceitfully. 3. With join consent: "We make it; we are all agreed in making it, and do it unanimously, that we may strengthen the hands one of another." 4. With fixed resolution: "It is a sure covenant, without reserving a power of revocation. It is what we will live and die by, and never go back from." A certain number of the princes, priests, and Levites, were chosen as the representatives of the congregation, to subscribe and seal it for and in the name of the rest. Now*

was fulfilled that promise concerning the Jews, that, when they returned out of captivity, they should join themselves to the Lord in a perpetual covenant (Jer. 50:5), and that in Isa. 44:5, that they should subscribe with their hand unto the Lord. He that bears an honest mind will not startle at assurances; nor will those that know the deceitfulness of their own hearts think them needless.

Structure of NT Church

Fourth, while the New Testament does not explicitly speak of a church covenant, there are some hints of it. The first suggestion of this is found in the Apostle Paul's desire to join himself to the church in Acts 9:26. "And when Saul was come to Jerusalem, he assayed to join himself to the disciples: but they were all afraid of him, and believed not that he was a disciple" (Acts 9:26). Here is an example of a person wanting to join the church. But they were cautious of him, not believing that he was a true disciple.

Let us note the word "joined."[18] This term is expressive of that strict union there is between the saints in church relation. It is used in Matthew 19:5 of the union between man and wife. In Luke 15:15, it speaks of the union between an employer and an apprentice. It literally has the idea of being glued together. This shows the close and intimate communion that Christians have with each other, and it importantly shows that their incorporation together is by mutual consent and agreement, as John Gill comments, "The phrase is expressive of that strict union there is between the saints in church relation, and of that close and intimate communion they have with each other, and shows that their incorporation together is by mutual consent and agreement." This is why the church covenant is so critical to the existence of any church.

Certainly, we can say that church membership in the New Testament times included an entry into covenantal relationship with God and with others. And this entrance is

---

[18] The imperfect form "assayed" suggests that he made repeated attempts to join himself, but the rest of the disciples were leery of his sincerity, thinking him to be a spy infiltrating their ranks.

symbolized by the ordinance of the baptism. A Christian is one baptized into Christ's death and life, and one also baptized into the body of Christ.[19] It really is the visible entrance into the covenant with God.

In 1 Tim. 6:12, Paul exhorts Timothy, "Fight the good fight of faith, lay hold on eternal life, whereunto thou art also called, and hast professed a good profession before many witnesses." The phrase "professed a good profession before many witnesses" is the language of covenant. Matthew Poole, therefore, states, that this profession is that "to which thou hast obliged thyself by covenant or promise, made either in thy baptism, or when thou wert set apart to thy ministry." On this Albert Barnes makes a fitting and relevant statement,

> *That is, either when he embraced the Christian religion, and made a public profession of it in the presence of the church and of the world; or when he was solemnly set apart to the ministry; or as he in his Christian life had been enabled publicly to evince his attachment to the Saviour. I see no reason to doubt that the apostle may have referred to the former, and that in early times a profession of religion may have been openly made before the church and the world. Such a method of admitting*

---

[19] 1 Corinthians 12:13. 'This has reference to the spiritual baptism, but the spiritual baptism is expressed in the water baptism; though they must be kept separate, seeing that one may be baptized without being truly united to Christ, as the baptism of Simon proves, yet they are connected as the symbol and reality. Hodge makes the following comment: No matter how great may have been the previous difference, whether they were Jews or Gentiles, bond or free, by this baptism of the Spirit, all who experience it are merged into one body; they are all intimately and organically united as partaking of the same life. Comp. Gal. 3:28. And this is the essential point of the analogy between the human body and the church. As the body is one because pervaded and animated by one soul or principle of life, so the church is one because pervaded by one Spirit. And as all parts of the body which partake of the common life belong to the body, so all those in whom the Spirit of God dwells are members of the church which is the body of Christ. And by parity of reasoning, those in whom the Spirit does not dwell are not members of Christ's body. They may be members of the visible or nominal church, but they are not members of the church in that sense in which it is the body of Christ. This passage, therefore, not only teaches us the nature of the church, but also the principle of its unity. It is one, not as united under one external visible head, or under one governing tribunal, nor in virtue of any external visible bond, but in virtue of the indwelling of the Holy Spirit in all its members. And this internal spiritual union manifests itself in the profession of the same faith, and in all acts of Christian fellowship.' –Charles Hodge.

members to the church would have been natural, and would have been fitted to make a deep impression on others. It is a good thing often to remind professors of religion of the feelings which they had when they made a profession of religion; of the fact that the transaction was witnessed by the world; and of the promises which they then made to lead holy lives. One of the best ways of stimulating ourselves or others to the faithful performance of duty, is the remembrance of the vows then made; and one of the most effectual methods of reclaiming a backslider is to bring to his remembrance that solemn hour when he publicly gave himself to God.

Then there is Peter's statement in 1 Peter 3:21, wherein he states, "The like figure whereunto *even* baptism doth also now save us (not the putting away of the filth of the flesh, but the answer of a good conscience toward God,) by the resurrection of Jesus Christ." The idea of "the answer of a good conscience toward God" is the central. John Gill explains this phrase in the following way:

The Vulgate Latin renders it, "the interrogation of a good conscience"; referring, it may be, to the interrogations that used to be put to those who desired baptism; as, dost thou renounce Satan? dost thou believe in Christ?, others render it, "the stipulation of a good conscience"; alluding also to the ancient custom of obliging those that were baptized to covenant and agree to live an holy life and conversation, to renounce the devil and all his works, and the pomps and vanities of this world; and baptism does certainly lay an obligation on men to walk in newness of life.

This is surely how the early church looked upon Baptism. Gregory of Nazianzen saw Baptism "as a covenant with God for a second life and purer conversation."[20] Chrysostom repeatedly refers to baptism as a contract, saying on one occasion, "This is

[20] Gregory Nazianzen, *Oration on Holy Baptism* VIII in *A Select Library of Nicene and Post-Nicene Fathers of the Christian Church.* 2nd series. (Peabody: Hendrickson Publishers, 1994), 7:362.

the signature; this the agreement; this the contract,"[21] wherein the Christian rejects Satan's domination and acknowledges Christ's sovereignty. And more recently, in 1675 Henry D'Anvers, an English Baptist, stated that "Baptism is no other, than our Mystical *Marriage* … and *striking* of a Covenant (the Essentials of Marriage) betwixt Christ and a believer."[22]

The Lord's Supper is also a covenantal ordinance. It is the renewal of the covenant. And this covenant is not merely with the Lord, but it speaks of a mutual binding and fellowship with one another.[23] We break the one loaf and partake, symbolizing our unity in Christ. We must forever see the Lord's Supper as a symbol of communion, a brotherly covenant among table companions.

The early church called the Lord's Supper a *sacramentum*, which means a soldier's pledge. Cyprian said that it was a pledge which fortified the Christian against Satan and his hosts. One theologian said this covenantal idea couched in the Lord's Supper, "The Lord's Supper [is] a covenant meal in which the Lordship of Christ and our commitment to do his will are brought again and again to the worshiping congregation."[24] One cannot understand the Lord's Supper apart from the covenant idea.

---

[21] John Chrysostom, *Baptismal Homily* 1. 16; 2. 17; 2. 18; 3. 20; in *Ancient Christian Writers*, (Paulist Press, 1962) 31:29, 50, 63.

[22] Henry D'Anvers, *A Treatise of Baptism* (London: Elephant and Castle, 1674), 216.

[23] 1 Corinthians 10:17. 'The design of the apostle is to show that every one who comes to the Lord's supper enters into communion with all other communicants. They form one body in virtue of their joint participation of Christ. This being the case, those who attend the sacrificial feasts of the heathen form one religious body. They are in religious communion with each other, because in communion with the demons on whom their worship terminates. Many distinguished commentators, however, prefer the following interpretation. "For we, though many, are one bread (and) one body." The participation of the same loaf makes us one bread, and the joint participation of Christ's body makes us one body. This is, to say the least, an unusual and harsh figure. Believers are never said to be one bread; and to make the ground of comparison the fact that the loaf is the joint product of many grains of wheat is very remote. And to say that we are literally one bread, because by assimilation the bread passes into the composition of the bodies of all the communicants, is to make the apostle teach modern physiology.' –Charles Hodge

[24] Dale Moody, "The Lord's Supper" (undated mimeographed essay), 5-6. Quoted by Deweese, 208.

Structure of Qumran Community

Fifth, though not biblical, the Qumran community clearly covenanted with one another. This shows that God's people from the earlier periods manifest a clear understanding that it is biblical to covenant one with another. I am sure that most –if not all—of you have heard of the Dead Sea Scroll, manuscripts found in caves on the west side of the Dead Sea, beginning in 1947. Scholars refer to these caves as the Qumran caves, after the Qumran community. This community was a strict sect of Essenes that remained loyal during days of great declension and may date back to the time of Antiochus Epiphanes (175-163 B.C.). In addition to the biblical texts that they left in their caves, they also left other documents about themselves. In these documents, we clearly find the idea of a community covenant. Speaking directly to the case of the Qumran community, Charles Deweese writes,

> *The covenant concept expressed itself in a special way in the context of initiation into the Qumran community. The Manual of Discipline has preserved two accounts of a ceremony of initiation. The first shows that persons joining the community covenanted to follow the commandments of God. In addressing "the obligation of holiness," the second states that*
>
> > *"Everyone who is admitted to the formal organization of the community is to enter into a covenant in the presence of all fellow-volunteers in the cause and to commit himself by a binding oath to abide with all his heart and soul by the commandments of the law of Moses. ..."*
>
> *Covenanters at Qumran received discipline when they failed to keep their pledges or violated the rules of the community. The most stringent discipline was exclusion, which resulted when a member of the community was found guilty of cursing God, complaining against the community, or lapsing after being in the community at least ten years.*

The Zadokite Document contains a section on the obligations of the covenant. After admonishing persons entering the covenant to live according to the injunctions of the law of God, the document lists sixteen injunctions, such as staying away from disreputable men, refraining from stealing, loving one's neighbor as oneself, and avoiding whoredom. God's covenant became effective for persons who lived these rules of holiness without failure. Persons pledging themselves to the injunctions of the law were not to depart from them even at the price of death. Also, the document mandates that parents within the covenant community should impose the oath of the covenant upon their sons when the sons reach the proper age.[25]

Now all of this speaks of the propriety of making covenants from the Jewish standpoint. It articulates the fact that the concept of the covenant is imbedded into the very nature of the Jewish mind. And it led them to make pacts with one another, binding one to another in their pursuit of God. This took place prior to the New Testament era.

Structure of the Ante-Nicene Church

Sixth, the ante-Nicene Christians clearly covenanted with one another But what about after the time wherein New Testament was written and the church established? Did Christians covenant one with another? We do discover the idea of the church covenant in the primitive and ante-Nicene church. During the reign of the Emperor Trajan (a. D. 98-117), we find a clear indication that believers were covenanting one with another. This fact is clearly manifested in the well-known letter of Pliny the Younger to the Emperor Trajan (written about the year A. D. 112), in which he says "that they [the Christians of that time in Pliny's domain] bound themselves by an oath at their meetings not to be guilty of theft, or robbery, or adultery, or the violation of their word or pledge."[26] They voluntarily entered into

[25] Deweese, 16-17.

covenants wherein people contract with one another to live in accordance to the faith and doctrine which they mutually profess.

Furthermore, we find another proof that the early church covenanted together from the life of Tertullian. Tertullian, who lived about the end of the second century, gives us the same account of the state, order, and worship of the churches. The description of a church he first lays down in these words, "We are a body in the conscience of religion by an agreement in discipline and in a covenant of hope" (*Apology, 39*).[27] Speaking in this statement by Tertullian, John Owen comments,

> *For whereas such a body or religious society could not be united but by a covenant, he calls it 'a covenant of hope;' because the principal respect was had therein unto the things hoped for. They covenanted together so to live and walk in the discipline of Christ, or obedience unto his commands, as that they might come together unto the enjoyment of eternal blessedness.*[28]

Throughout the Bible, we that the covenant is central, and it binds God to men, men to God, and men to one another. Central to it all is the idea that a covenant is central is forming a religious community. It is central is forming a body that has a certain confession and practice. When we come to the New Testament, this is voluntarily entered into. This is how both the Jews and the

---

[26] The part of Pliny's letter referring to the point in hand reads in the Latin, *"Segue sacramento non in scelus aliquod obstringere, sed nefurta, ne latrocinia, ne adulteria committerent, ne fidem fallerent, ne depositum appellati abnegarent"* (*C. Plinii Caecelii Secunfii Epistolarum Libri Decent et Panegyricus. Parisiis. 1823. Epistola XcVII.*, pp. 199, 200). This Is quoted in Champlin Burrage, *The Covenant Idea: Its Origin and Its Development* (Philadelphia: American Baptist Publication Society, 1904), x.

[27] Tertullian, *Apology*, 39, in *Ante-Nicene Fathers* (Peabody: Hendrickson Publications, 1994), volume 3. "*Corpus sumus de conscientia religionis, et discipline divinitate, et spei foedere.*" As Henry Martyn Dexter notes, 'This is misquoted by John Wise, who adds "whereas such a body, or religious society, could not be united but by a covenant; he (Tertullian) calls it a covenant of hope, because the principal respect therein was had unto the things hoped for." —*John Wise's "Vindication."* p. 8, Ed. 1772,' in Dexter, *Congregationalism: What it is; Whence it is; How it works* (Boston: Boyles, Holmes, and Company, 1874), 29.

[28] John Owen, "An Inquiry into the Original, Nature, Institution, Power, Order, and Communion of Evangelical Churches," in *The Works of John Owen*, XV: 297.

early Church perceived the basis of the unity between those of like precious faith.

The Organizing Structure of the Church Covenant

Now, let us turn to the structure of the modern church covenants. Historically speaking, the actual content was normally comprised of at least four distinct categories: church fellowship, church discipline, public worship and personal devotion, and pastoral and congregational care. The way in which church covenants address these issues varies.

Our covenant does deal with all of these points, but it is not do so under these normal categories. Our categories would be commitment to church fellowship, commitment to public worship, commitment to domestic and personal holiness, and commitment to mutual edification. Let us consider each of these briefly.

The Theme of Fellowship

The first category centers on the theme of fellowship. The concept of mutual fellowship consists primarily in the fact that we give ourselves up to the Lord and to one another. In essence, this focuses upon the very constitution of a church. It is the voluntary, mutual biding of hearts to seek the Lord. The words are solemn but joyful. The words of our covenant reflect this trend:

> *Having been led by the Holy Spirit to receive the Lord Jesus Christ as our Savior (John 3:6,16), and on the public confession of our faith (Heb. 10:22-23), having been baptized in the name of the Father, and of the Son, and of the Holy Spirit (Matt. 28:19 20), we do now, in the presence of God and this assembly, solemnly and joyfully enter covenant with one another, as an expression of the one body in Christ (Acts 2:46).*

The Theme of Worship

The second category centers on the theme of worship. Public worship and personal devotion comprised the third area of covenantal concern. Church members committed themselves to worship together on Sunday and at other times. We promise to encourage and support the preaching of the gospel. We pledged to participate in celebrating the Lord's Supper. The words of the covenant call us to maintain and spread the mutual faith that we share. Our covenant reads,

> *We purpose, therefore, by the aid of the Holy Spirit (Eph. 5:18), to walk together in Christian love (Eph. 5:2), to strive for the advancement of the Church in knowledge, holiness and peace (Col. 1:10; I Thess. 4:3; Eph. 4:3), to promote its prosperity and spirituality (Acts 2:47), to attend its services regularly (Heb. 10:24), to sustain its worship (I Tim. 2:1-2), ordinances (Matt. 28:19-20), discipline (II Thess. 3:14-15), and doctrine (Titus 2:1); to give it a sacred preeminence over all institutions of human origin (I Cor. 3:17), to give faithfully of time and talent in its activities (Eph. 5:16; I Pet. 4:10-11), to contribute cheerfully and regularity (II Cor. 9:7), as God has prospered us (I Cor. 16:2), to the support of the ministry (I Tim, 5:17-18), the relief of the poor (II Cor. 8:4), and the spread of the Gospel throughout all nations (I Cor. 9:4-7).*

The Theme of Domestic and Personal Holiness

The third category centers on the theme of domestic and personal holiness. This really is at the heart of the covenant for it calls us all to live a life that adorns the gospel. It takes the doctrines which we share and fleshes it out, making it practical to our individual lives. It speaks of family and private worship, the duty to train our children in the Lord, and the responsibility to live as lights in this evil world. Our covenant here reads,

> *We also purpose to maintain family and private worship (Dan. 9:4-19), to train our children according to the Word of God (Deut. 6:4-9), to walk carefully in the world (Eph. 5:15; Col. 4:5), to be just in our dealings (I Pet. 2:12), faithful in our engagements (I Cor. 4:2), and exemplary in our conduct (I Cor. 11:1), to avoid all gossip (I Tim. 5:13),*

speaking that which is evil (I Pet. 2:12), and unrighteous anger (Eph. 4:31), to abstain from all forms of activity which dishonor our Lord Jesus Christ (I Cor. 10:31), cause stumbling to a fellow believer (I Cor. 8:9) or hinder the winning of a soul to Christ (I Cor. 10:27-28), to be zealous in our efforts to advance the cause of Christ, our Savior (II Cor. 5:20), and to give Him preeminence in all things (Col. 1:12-13).

The Theme of Mutual Responsbility

The last category centers on the theme of our mutual responsibility to concern ourselves with others. It calls us to encourage one another, pray for one another, and watch over one another. At the center of this category is the idea of possessing a mutual love for one another. On this, our covenant reads,

> *We further purpose to encourage one another in the blessed hope of our Lord's return (I Thess. 4:13-5:11; Titus 2:13), to watch over one another in brotherly love (I Thess. 3:12), to remember each other in prayer (Jas. 5:14-18), to aid each other in sickness and distress (II Cor. 1:8-11), to cultivate Christian sympathy in feelings and courtesy in speech (Eph. 4:32,29), to be slow to take offense,(Jas.1: 19-20), but always ready for reconciliation (Col. 3:13).*

Moreover, the structure and content of the church covenant need not be static. The covenant may stress things of contemporary importance. For example, I spoke with one church that has placed statements opposed to abortion and homosexuality within it. I have also seen church covenants highlighting the biblical teaching on the family. Another example is found in the practice among many churches in covenanting against pornography.

A cursory look at the language used, the numerous biblical references, or the issues addressed with reveal that the covenant is essentially biblical in its focus. There is an effort to call us to an evangelical obedience, not a placing of a legalistic yoke of unbiblical burdens upon the back of God's people. In this, it is really nothing more than a covenant indicating that we are agreed to live in the light of biblical truth. There is only one source of faith and practice –the Bible. The covenant seeks merely to summarize and set forth an interpretation of the biblical duties incumbent upon true Christians in association with one another. In one old church covenant, the biblical emphasis is put in verse form:

New rules we do no mean to make,

The Bible rules we only take,

And shew by this our script'ral creed,

In Bible truth we are agreed.

The Practical Impact of the Church Covenant

Throughout this brief discussion of the church covenant, we have asserted that the church covenant is an integral and significant part of our church life. But how is it integral and significant? Or, we may put this in a different way: how should it have an integral and significant role in our church life. This is not a small issue seeing that we have said that the form of our visible organization is rooted in the covenant. It is that which officially and formally binds us one to another in the Lord. By the means of the covenant, the regenerate members of this church says, "Here is the local church to which I belong, and this is this people to which I give my heart in mutual affection, worship and fellowship in the Gospel."29 Let us trace this in the life of the church.

The Church Covenant and Membership

Every true believer should join a church. As he does, he immediately assumes responsibilities. These responsibilities encompass his relationship to God, to the church, and to the world. The covenant outlines these, acting as a summary of the evangelical ethic found primarily in the New Testament. These duties are integral to personal discipleship; they are fundamental to the nature of the church; they are vital to its health; and they are central to its mission. As such the covenant cannot be treated casually. It must not be ignored. It calls us to a life of service to God, the church, and to the world. Speaking of this, Charles W. Deweese rightly asserts,

> *The accomplishing of such ministries and disciplines as regular attendance in Bible study and worship, responsible stewardship, sensitive caring, and exemplary*

---

[29] As John Gill correctly remarks, "It is this confederacy, consent, and agreement, that is the formal cause of a church; it is this which not only distinguishes a church from the world, but from all other particular churches; so the church at Cenchrea was not the same with the church at Corinth, though but at a little distance from it. Onesimus and Epaphras were of the church at Collosse, and not of another, Col. iv. 9. 12" See Appendix for his comments on the mutual agreement between believers.

living is foundational to committed discipleship. Careful use of a covenant is one way to help assure that these and other ministries and disciplines will become fully activated and effective. Perhaps the best approach to covenantal practices is one that is continuing and comprehensive for all members. Church members of all ages should sense the gravity of covenantal pledges and the need to live up to the biblical principles that support them. A church will do well to place on its present members the same covenantal expectations that it intends to present to future members. Failure to do this will create a double standard of ethics for members and falsify the legitimacy of covenanting as being applicable to the whole church. Covenantal practices require full participation by all members. [30]

Upon joining this church, the covenant helps to articulate the biblical expectations for the new member. It calls him to live in light of the gospel. It must be remembered that the church is not merely a democracy wherein the majority agree to pursue a certain course. It is, in the words of Lindsay, a "theocratic democracy":

But the authority which the Church possesses is altogether different from what a voluntary association of men may exercise upon its members, and of another kind from what is possessed by lawful civil government. The authority comes from Christ Himself. The Christian Democracy is also a Theocracy; it combines the two ideas of rule associated with the Greek and the Hebrew uses of the word "ecclesia." While the authority belongs to the whole membership, and is therefore democratic; it nevertheless comes from above, and is therefore theocratic. It comes from Jesus Christ, who is the Head of the Church.

When these expectations are ignored or displaced by either the person or the church, then there are serious

---

[30] Charles W. Deweese, *Baptist Church Covenants* (Nashville, Broadman Press, 1990), 207.

implications. Mark Dever, in his excellent little book *Nine Marks of a Healthy Church*, puts his finger on the issue:

> *If the church is a building, then we must be bricks in it; if the church is a body, then we are its members; if the church is the household of faith, then we are part of that household. Sheep are in a flock, and branches on a vine. Biblically, if we are Christians we must be members of a church. This membership is not simply the record of a statement we once made or of affection toward a familiar place. It must be a reflection of a living commitment or it is worthless.*
>
> *Worse than being worthless, it is dangerous. Uninvolved members confuse both real members and non-Christians about what it means to be a Christian. We "active" members do the voluntarily "inactive" members no service when we allow them to remain members of the church. Membership is the church's corporate endorsement of a person's salvation. Yet how can a congregation honestly testify that someone invisible to it is faithfully running the race?*[31]

Let me follow up the last quote with another from Ryken's *The Communion of Saints*. In this section the author is arguing for the importance of belonging to a specific local church.

> *The same might be said of regular attenders who never join the church. They lack an unbreakable commitment to the church and its ministry. Nonmembers, however active they may be in the life of the church, are outside the covenant relationship with the body of Christ that God requires. They reserve the right to pick and choose their doctrine, lifestyle, and ministry. In effect they become their own elders denying the authority of the church to carry out its mandate of gathering and perfecting the saints. To put this in theological terms, they separate*

[31] Mark Dever, *Nine Marks of a Healthy Church* (Wheaton, IL: Crossway, 2004), 162-63.

union with Christ, the head of the church, from union with his body. As a result, they confuse themselves and others - outside as well as inside the church - about what it means to be a Christian. This is a costly mistake to make because membership has its privileges. Martyn Lloyd-Jones went so far as to describe church membership as 'the biggest honour which can come a man's way in this world.' There is no union with Christ apart from the communion of the saints. Nor can the saints have true communion without belonging to one another by belonging to Christ in his church. The communion of the saints is for members only.[32]

The Church Covenant and the Lord's Supper

Now, having been admitted into the church, we begin to worship in the church. One of the central aspects of the church's worship is the Lord's Supper. Each time that we partake of the Lord's Supper with each other, the Lord is summoning us to renew our covenant to Him and to one to another. We should be doing this every time that we have the Lord's Supper. In a real and definite sense, the covenantal idea is foundational to all the other meanings of the Lord's Supper.

It is of great interest to me that Baptist history is filled with examples of churches using covenants in the setting of the Lord's Supper. Even church covenant meetings, which flourished among Baptists in the 1800s, were intended to prepare church members for participation in the Lord's Supper. The Lord's Supper is a covenantal meal, and it calls us to renew our dedication to the privileges and obligations of the New Covenant. And in this it calls us to realize that we are one body. One cannot come to the Lord's Supper and see it as something that reflects is attachment to Christ. He must see it as something that reflects his attachment to all others in the church. *"We who are many are one body: for we all partake of the one bread" 1 Cor. 10: 17.* Speaking of this, Andrew Murray wrote,

---

[32] Philip Graham Ryken, *The Communion of Saints: Living in Fellowship with the People of God* (P & R Publishing, 2001), 55.

Union with the Lord Jesus, the Head, involves at the same time mutual union with the members of the body. He that really eats the body of Jesus and drinks His blood, is incorporated with His body, and stands thenceforth in the closest relationship to the whole body, with all its members. We have fellowship, not only in His body which He gave up to death, but especially in His body which He brought again from the dead—that is, the Church. "We are one body; for we all partake of the one bread."

So deep and wonderful was this union of His believing disciples at the table of the New Covenant, so entirely new the life of the Spirit by which they were to be gathered together into one in Him as His body, that the Lord spoke of the love which must animate them as a new commandment. In the New Covenant there was present a new life, and thus also a new love. "By this shall all men know that ye are My disciples, if ye have love one to another."[33]

This is really the focus of Paul in addressing the Corinthians in his first letter. There were great divisions among them, and he was saying that these are contrary and in opposition to the very nature of the covenantal meal. We renew our covenant with the Lord Himself, but in doing so, we (by necessity) renew it among ourselves. Therefore, it is of a very practical necessity that we see the Lord's Supper as covenantal in nature. Speaking of this, Ralph Wardlaw, in his work *Congregational Independency,* states,

That in some Christian bodies there are not a few who become communicants, without having any notion of communion, who, when they come to the Lord's table, think of no fellowship but that of their own souls individually with their gracious Redeemer, is a position which none will question who know the state of the facts. Of spiritual union with those who come with them to the same table, they never think, and have never, or hardly

---

[33] Andrew Murray, *The Lord's Table* (Chicago: Fleming Revell, 1897), 96.

ever, been taught to think. Even when this is the case, there cannot fail to be a great deficiency in the working out of the ends of Christian fellowship;—a fellowship which, according to the New Testament, includes the reciprocal exercise of all those social affections that spring from the consideration of the number and the power of the bonds of union,—the "one body, and one spirit, and one hope of their calling, the one Lord, one faith, one baptism, one God and Father of all, who is above all, and through all, and in them all,"—and which includes also the practical result of these affections, in "all the members having the same care one of another," —"every man looking, not on his own things, but also on the things of others."[34]

In reality, the Lord's Supper helps the Christian community renew the vows made in baptism. If a church celebrates the Lord's Supper in the same worship service in which it baptizes new members, then the covenantal themes of the two ordinances can be tied together. The Lord's Super will and should regularly remind the congregation of its covenant pledges. At the Lord's Supper, each member should take up the prayer of J. J. Janeway,

And now, blessed God, admiring thine infinite condescension, and sensible of my great unworthiness, I come, invited by thee, to renew that covenant, in which I have taken the Father, Son, and Holy Ghost, to be my God and portion for ever; and in which I have given myself to thee, as thy rightful property, to be thy obedient servant and loving child, forever and ever. I engage in this wonderful transaction, relying on thy grace to help me to fulfil my engagements. Grant me, 0 my God and Father, the aids of thy Spirit, that I may be faithful to my covenant engagements, until death. And to the Father, Son, and Holy Ghost, be eternal praise and glory. Amen![35]

---

[34] Ralph Wardlaw, *Congregational Independency* (Glasgow: James Maclehose, 1864), 128.

[35] Jacob Jones Janeway, *The Communicant's Manual* (Philadelphia: Presbyterian Board of Publications, 1848), 139.

The Church Covenant and Church Life

At the core of the New Testament concept of the church is the idea that the church is made up of regenerate men and women. The New Testament is different from the Old Testament in this regard. In the Old Testament, there were many within the external covenant that were never part of the internal covenant. "For they are not all Israel, which are of Israel," as Paul said (Romans 9:6). But in the New Covenant, every person shall all know the Lord in truth, "from the least of them unto the greatest of them, saith the LORD" (Jeremiah 31:34). John S. Hammett comments on this issue, as it relates to his own denomination.

> *History records that though regenerate church membership was at the heart of the origin of Baptists and was for most of Baptist history central to Baptist ecclesiology, it dramatically declined in Baptist life in the twentieth century and is in desperate need of recovery today.. . .*
>
> *Today, a denomination like the Southern Baptist Convention maintains the theology of regenerate church membership in its official statements, but in reality, its churches show little evidence of regeneration in the behavior of their members. It is widely known that divorce and moral problems are as common among church members as nonchurch members. Even the very modest index of attendance at Sunday morning worship shows close to two-thirds of Southern Baptist church members missing on any given Sunday morning. Regenerate church membership cannot be seriously maintained as characterizing most Baptist churches in North America today.*[36]

One of the means to maintain a regenerate body of believers in this or any other church is a consistent emphasis and practice of the church covenant. From the time of admitting new members, this church must continually and comprehensively

[36] John S. Hammett, "Regenerate Church Membership" in *Restoring Integrity in Baptist Churches*, edited by Thomas White, Jason G. Duesing, and Malcolm B. Yarnell III (Grand Rapids: Kregel, 2008), 23-27.

demand that all of its members live in the light of its obligations as summarily comprehended in the church covenant. The entire congregation must insist that each member fully participate to his fullest ability, exercising his gifts as the Lord has given to profit the whole body.

Immediately, a number of issues come to the front. To begin with, we must not employ the church covenant legalistically. Certainly, one can be brow-beaten into submitting to the external duties outlined in the covenant. And a person's spirituality may even be judged by his external conformity to the covenant stipulations, though his heart is far from the Lord. This is a sad truth, and it must be combated. The heart of all true worship and service is the heart that is in love with God and serving out of gratitude for redemption through Christ's blood. The love of Christ must constrain us, and the mercies of God must be the ground for our reasonable service and worship to God.

However, at the same time, we must vehemently reject the idea that the mere calling of men to live biblically is a form of legalism. In our day, wherein myriads kick against all authority and are imbibed with antinomian sentiments, we will often meet with such resistance. In this case, we must follow the advice of Paul in Tit. 2:15: "These things speak, and exhort, and rebuke with all authority. Let no man despise thee."[37]

In addition, we must guard ourselves against establishing a double standard. Every member of this church should be held responsible for doing all that he or she can do to meet the requirements in the covenant. Both young and old members must be held to the same standard. Partiality and favoritism have no part here. And both present members as well as future members should be held to the same code of ethics. "A church will do well to place on its present members the same covenantal expectations

---

[37] "This conclusion is of the same meaning as if he enjoined Titus to dwell continually on that doctrine of edification, and never to grow weary, because it cannot be too much inculcated. He likewise bids him add the spurs of "exhortations and reproofs;" for men are not sufficiently admonished as to their duty, if they be not also vehemently urged to the performance of it. He who understands those things which the Apostle has formerly stated, and who has them always in his mouth, will have ground not only for teaching, but likewise for correcting." –Calvin.

that it intends to present to future members. Failure to do this will create a double standard of ethics for members and falsify the legitimacy of covenanting as being applicable to the whole church."[38]

Also, we must beware of a false standard. Certainly wisdom must be used to discern whether or not one is conforming to the standards. A shut-in or one with medical issues cannot possibly meet the stipulations of attendance as he possibly would like. To expect him to do so is unfair and ungodly. Yet, we must not tolerate any one's effort to leverage such an exceptional failure as an excuse to absence himself when the church meets. In his *Manual of Church Order*, the venerable John Dagg gives us the following wise advice.

> *The duty of every individual church is, to press toward the mark, for the prize of the high calling of God in Christ Jesus; and the duty of every church, and of every church member, is, to strive in every lawful way for church perfection. Though full perfection may not be attained, yet approach to it sufficiently rewards our continual effort; and, apart from all respect to reward, we are obliged to this course, by the command of Christ.*[39]

The covenant is something that should run through the entire life of our congregation. Since the covenant is that which acts as the formal basis for the church, it should be the backdrop of the church's life. Addressing this, one of the leading scholars on Baptist Covenants wrote, "Church members of all ages should sense the gravity of covenantal pledges and the need to live up to the biblical principles that support them."[40]

The Church Covenant and Discipline

Church covenants have long been associated with church discipline. This discipline may be corrective, reformative discipline, but its primary focus should be formative and

---

[38] Charles W. Deweese, *Baptist Church Covenants* (Nashville, Broadman Press, 1990), 207.

[39] John L. Dagg, *Manual of Church Order, (Harrisonburg, VA: Gano Books, 1990), 98.*

[40] Deweese, *Baptist Church Covenants,* 207.

instructive discipline. Both are sorely needed in our churches. R. Albert Molher, Jr. has rightly said,

> *The decline of church discipline is perhaps the most visible failure of the contemporary church. No longer concerned with maintaining purity of confession or lifestyle, the contemporary church sees itself as a voluntary association of autonomous members, with minimal moral accountability to God, much less to each other.*[41]

This is a fatal flaw. Since the time of the Reformation, the Church has identified proper discipline as an essential mark of the true church. Simply put, no true Church can exist, if church discipline does not exist. The 1561 Belgic Confession articulates the essential marks of a true Church in the following way:

> *The marks by which the true Church is known are these: If the pure doctrine of the gospel is preached therein; if she maintains the pure administration of the sacraments as instituted by Christ; if church discipline is exercised in punishing of sin; in short, if all things are managed according to the pure Word of God, all things contrary thereto rejected, and Jesus Christ acknowledged as the only Head of the Church. Hereby the true Church may certainly be known, from which no man has a right to separate himself.*[42]

If we allow our church to run as "a voluntary association of autonomous members, with minimal moral accountability to God, much less to each other," the entire church's health will be put into jeopardy, and the mission of the church will come to a halt. By definition, the church is a number of regenerate men and women in association by covenant. If discipline is ignored or not practiced, unregenerate men and women will come into the church. The covenant helps mitigate this, calling men and

---

[41] R. Albert Mohler, "Church Discipline: The Missing Mark," Chapter 8 in *The Compromised Church: The Present Evangelical Crisis*©, John H. Armstrong, General Editor. [Wheaton, Ill.: Crossway Books, 1998].

[42] "The Belgic Confession," in *The Creeds of Christendom*, ed. Philip Schaff, rev. David S. Schaff, Vol. 3 (New York: Harper and Row, 1931), pp. 419-420.

women to both a right profession and a proper life. Both the right profession and the right behavior are vital, as Mark Dever explains,

> *The idea that membership in a local church should only require a profession of faith in Christ is an idea that is both common and destructive to the life and witness of the church. Historically, Baptists have realized that any profession of faith should be tried and deemed credible. After all, a saving profession of faith includes repentance. A Christian life will be revealed not only by participation in baptism and the Lord's Supper but also by regular attendance at the congregation's gatherings, and a submission to the discipline of the congregation. This includes regular praying for the congregation and tithing. When congregations do not give attention to lifestyles of repentance, nominal Christianity quickly comes to characterize the church to the world, hurt its witness, and lie about the character of God."*[43]

One of the key areas wherein the church covenant helps is found in its biblical stipulation that each member be actively involved in the life of our congregation. However, in our day, when each man does that which is right in his own eyes, nonattendance is epidemic. This is merely another symptom of the view that the church is "a voluntary association of autonomous members, with minimal moral accountability to God, much less to each other." People cannot be permitted to attend according to their caprice, as Mark Dever elsewhere explains,

> *A member's regular, tolerated nonattendance begins to raise further questions. What kind of leadership must a church have to allow such a misrepresentation to arise and flourish? What expectations are being communicated to those who are joining? What discipline is practiced, if any? In fact, tolerated noninvolvement among members may even call into question the kind of evangelism being done and the church's understanding of conversion, even*

---

[43] Mark E. Dever, "The Church" in *A Theology for the Church,* edited by Daniel L. Akin (Nashville: Broadman & Holman, 2007).

of the gospel itself. Allowing such nonattending members to retain their membership would seem to be such blatant disobedience to Scripture, and such a brazen disregard of the scriptural health of those concerned, that it would even call into question the teaching that brought about such an unhealthy tolerance in the body.[44]

Many objections have been made to this use of covenants. One of the most common objections is that the covenant must be interpreted by fallible men who may be too lenient or too severe. Well, this is sadly true. This simply cannot be denied. History is replete with examples of this type of abuse and neglect. While we dare not deny it, we can seek to give a correct response to it. There are two things to say in response to this.

On one hand, the entire congregation is the one who decides these matters, and the Lord has promised that when the church meets in this regard, "For where two or three are gathered together in my name, there am I in the midst of them" (Matt. 18:20). It is not simply a matter between the elders and the allegedly guilty person, but it involves the entire congregation with the Lord guiding them.[45] Speaking on this, J. C. Ryle made these sagacious remarks,

It is vain to deny that the whole subject is surrounded with difficulties. On no point has the influence of the world weighed so heavily on the action of Churches. On no point have Churches made so many mistakes,—sometimes on the side of sleepy remissness, sometimes on the side of blind severity. No doubt the power of excommunication has been fearfully abused and perverted, and, as Quesnel says, "we ought to be more afraid of our sins than of all the excommunications in the world." Still it is impossible to deny, with such a passage as this before us, that church discipline is according to

---

[44] Mark Dever, "Regaining Meaningful Church Membership" in *Restoring Integrity in Baptist Churches*, edited by Thomas White, Jason G. Duesing, and Malcolm B. Yarnell III (Grand Rapids: Kregel, 2008), 46.

[45] This does not mean that all councils are infallible. Many do not hold to the faith of Christ; therefore, they do not meet in His name, as Calvin reminds us "But we ought first of all to inquire whether those persons, as to whose faith, and doctrine, and dispositions, we are in doubt, were *assembled in the name of Christ.*"

the mind of Christ, and, when wisely exercised, is calculated to promote a church's health and well-being. It can never be right that all sorts of people, however wicked and ungodly, should be allowed to come to the table of the Lord, no man letting or forbidding. It is the bounden duty of every Christian to use his influence to prevent such a state of things. A perfect communion can never be attained in this world, but purity should be the mark at which we aim. An increasingly high standard of qualification for full church-membership, will always be found one of the best evidences of a prosperous church.[46]

On the other hand, we may reply that, while the congregation is filled with fallible judges, it is the congregation's duty to judge. We are to judge those within the congregation (1 Corinthians 5:12, 13). We have a moral responsibility both to the offender and to the entire church. To the offender, we owe him our love to correct him and admonish him with the greatest of affection and desire for restoration. To the congregation, we owe our effort to hinder the spread of leaven within the body. John L. Dagg comments,

The churches are not infallible judges, being unable to search the heart; but they owe it to the cause of Christ, and to the candidate himself, to exercise the best judgment of which they are capable. To receive any one on a mere profession of words, without any effort to ascertain whether he understands and feels what he professes, is unfaithfulness to his interest, and the interests of religion.[47]

Surely, this church needs wisdom as she enforces her church covenant. At times, she may feel very insufficient for the task to which she is called. Yet the Lord has promised to be present, "presiding over them, ruling in their hearts, directing their counsels, assisting them in all they are concerned, confirming what they do, and giving a blessing and success to all

---

[46] Ryle, *Expository Thoughts on the Gospel: Matthew* (New York: Robert Carter and Brothers, 1870), 226.

[47] John L. Dagg, *Manual of Church Order*, 269.

they are engaged in."[48] She may look at her numbers and fear that any effort to enforce the agreed upon covenant is suicide, but God has not given her the spirit of fear, but of power, and of love, and of a sound mind. She must look to the Lord for wisdom. Deweesse gives some sound advice here.

> *Come to terms with frequently raised objections to a disciplined church membership. Avoid the extreme of converting church discipline into legalism. Take discipline seriously in order to make it successful. State the church's disciplines in a written covenant. Construct church discipline on a solidly biblical basis. View discipline as the task of the entire congregation. Place primary emphasis on the formative phase of discipline, rather than on the corrective. Assist a wayward member best by helping him or her solve a problem, not by excluding the person from membership, although exclusion does have a biblical basis and may be necessary in extreme situations. Apply corrective church discipline with therapeutic intentions and with the hope of redemption and reconciliation, or not at all. Baptists have tended to maintain a close relationship between church discipline and church covenants. Each church needs to arrive at its own understanding of how to relate the two today. A written covenant can identify key nurturing disciplines of church life, such as participation in worship, prayer, Bible study, giving of money, service, and witness. In a covenant these and other disciplines are placed before the congregation in baptism, the Lord's Supper, and other settings. The disciplines can eventually occupy a prominent place in the lives of members. The disciplinary value of a covenant exists mainly in an alliance with preventive discipline rather than with reformative discipline, although, at times, the latter is essential, too. The covenantal practice of providing disciplines by which church members can live out their Christian commitments most meaningfully deserves to be restored for the advantage of the church and its members.*

---

[48] John Gill, *Exposition on the Entire Bible*, *Loc. Cit.*

Since discipline in its preventive and corrective applications is an essential guardian of the regenerate quality of church life, a healthy reunion of discipline and covenants in Baptist life may lead to church renewal.[49]

Fundamentally, there is a one essential question that must be answered. Do the stipulations within the church covenant reflect the evangelical duties of the New Testament? If so, the obligation to obey remains binding, regardless if a person balks at it. Therefore, it is criminal for the congregation to ignore its responsibilities because of the fear of men. What has been worth writing down is worth keeping because it reflects the mind of God. But when someone does not want to keep it, then it is the mind of God to correct them for the welfare of that individual's soul as well as the welfare of the entire church. Thus, our church covenant is also worth preserving by means of church discipline.

The Church Covenant and Revival

The covenant renewal has been closely associated with revival. This is certainly the case in the Old Testament, but it is also the case in modern history. There is a real reason for this, as Dagg explains, "Churches are often criminally careless, both in the reception of members, and in the discipline of them when received. If the piety of churches were very fervent, men of cold hearts could not remain happy among them, and could not continue to have their true character concealed."[50] For this reason, church covenants have had a twofold relationship to revival. They have been harbingers, revealing that God is working in hearts, calling them back to Himself and to His ways. But they are also byproduct of revivals, when revived men renew their covenants before the Lord.

Let me provide an example of this from the history of New England. The early years of Salem's history were filled with contention and strife. The coming and going of Roger Williams especially left the congregation in a sidetracked condition. However, under the gifted leadership of Hugh Peters, the church

---

[49] Deweese, *Baptist Church Covenants*, 209.

[50] - John L. Dagg, *Manual of Church Order*, 99.

took on new life and increased in numbers. One of his first acts was to lead the church to a solemn renewal of the covenant of 1629. This was enlarged greatly by nine new articles dealing more or less with questions which had arisen in connection with the disturbance occasioned by Williams. The opening words are very characteristic and give a pattern widely followed,

> *Wee whose names are here under written, members of the present church of Christ in Salem, having found by sad experience how dangerous it is to sitt loose to the Covenant wee made with our God; and how apt wee are to wander into bypathes, even to the looseing of our first aimes in entring into Church fellowship: Doe therefore solemnly .... renewe that church Covenant we find this Church bound unto.*[51]

One of the grounds to the Great Awakening was the call to a covenant renewal by Cotton Mather and other ministers. And Jonathan Edwards called his people to renew their covenant at the height of the revival. At the close of this book *Treatise Concerning Religious Affections*, there was a lengthy reference to the covenant. This concerned not the Covenant of Grace but the church-covenant. Thus he sought to emphasize the necessity of true covenanting from the heart rather than the external form found in so many of the churches in his day.

> *God's people swearing to God, and swearing by his name, or to his name, as it might be rendered (by which seems to be signified their solemnly giving up themselves to him in covenant, and vowing to receive him as their God, and to be entirely his, to obey and serve him), is spoken of as a duty to be performed by all God's visible Israel, Deut. 6:13, and 10:20 , Psal. 63:11, Isa. 19:18, chap. 14:23, 24, compared with Rom. 14:11 , and Phil. 2:10, 11, Isa. 48:1, 2, and 65:15, 16, Jer. 4:2, and 5:7, and 12:16 , Hos. 4:16 , and 10:4. Therefore, in order to persons being entitled to full esteem and charity, with their neighbours, as being sincere professors of Christianity; by those*

---

[51] C. H. Webber and W. S. Nevins, *Old Naumkeag: An Historical Sketch of Salem* (Massachusetts: Smith and Company, 1877). 32f,

forementioned rules of Christ and his apostles, there must be a visibly holy life, with a profession, either expressing, or plainly implying such things as those which have been now mentioned. We are to know them by their fruits, that is, we are by their fruits to know whether they be what they profess to be; not that we are to know by their fruits, that they have something in them, they do not so much as pretend to.[52]

This does not mean that revival can be produced by renewing an outward conformity to this or to ANY document. However, it does mean that, when the people of God are serious about their covenant obligation, God is working in them to will and do His good pleasure. No revival is God-sent that does not lead His people to fulfill their covenant obligations to Him and to fellow Christians. Vitality in the church is only seen in loving obedience to the Lord and loving service to others.

---

[52] Jonathan Edwards, *A Treatise Concerning Religious Affections* (Philadelphia: James Crissy, 1821), 378.

Conclusion

In 1663 Richard Alleine published Vindiciae Pietatis: or, *A Vindication of Godliness in the Greater Strictness and Spirituality of It.*[53] In 1753, it was again published in John Wesley's *A Christian Library.* Wesley used one chapter, "The Application of the Whole," on Monday, August 11, 1755, in what probably was the first real celebration of the Covenant Service in the Methodist movement.

John Wesley remembered the vows that he made in a covenant to the Lord with others. In 1755, he wrote a Covenant Prayer. Possibly, we can make that prayer ours this day. Possibly, we can renew our commitment one to another.

I am no longer my own, but yours.
Put me to what you will, rank me with whom you will;
Put me to doing, put me to suffering.
Let me be employed for you or laid aside for you,

Exalted for you or brought low for you.
Let me be full, let me be empty;
Let me have all things, let me have nothing;
I freely and heartily yield all things to your pleasure and disposal.

And now, O glorious and blessed God,
Father, Son and Holy Spirit,
You are mine, and I am yours. So be it.
And the covenant which I have made on earth,
Let it be ratified in heaven. Amen.

Wesley found the covenant services rich and meaningful, as expressed in his Journal: "Many mourned before God, and many were comforted" (April 1756); "It was, as usual, a time of remarkable blessing" (October 1765); "It was an occasion for a variety of spiritual experiences ... I do not know that ever we had a greater blessing. Afterwards many desired to return thanks,

---

[53] A Puritan and brother of his more famous brother Joseph Allein –the author of *Alarm to the Uncoverted,*

either for a sense of pardon, for full salvation, or for a fresh manifestation of His graces, healing all their backslidings" (January 1, 1775).[54] May we renew our covenant with the Lord, and may He be pleased to bless us as we commit ourselves to Him and to one another for Jesus' sake.

---

[54] Wesley, *The Works of the Rev. John Wesley, A. M.* 4th Edition (London: John Mason, 1829), 2:361; 3:241; and 4:39.

Appendix A: "The nature of a Gospel Church, the Seat of Public Worship"

By John Gill

Gill's Complete Body of Practical and Doctrinal Divinity, Abridged by William Staughton, D. D. (Philadelphia: Wm. B. Graves, 1810), 514f.

A particular church may be considered as to the form of it; which lies in mutual consent and agreement in their covenant and consideration with each other.

1. There must be an union, a coalition of a certain number of persons to form a church state, one cannot make a church; and these must be united, as the similes of a tabernacle, temple, house, body, and a flock of sheep to which a church is sometimes compared, show; one curtain did not make a tabernacle, an human body is not one member, but many; one sheep does not make a flock, nor two or three straggling ones; but a number of them collected together feeding in one pasture, under the care of a shepherd.

2. This union of saints in a church state, is signified by their being joined, and as it were glued together; and it becomes members to endeavour to *keep the unity of the Spirit in the bond of peace,* Acts iv. 32. Col. ii. 2. Eph. iv. 3.

3. This union between them is made by voluntary consent and agreement.

4. As the original constitution of churches is by consent and confederation, so the admission of new members to them, is upon the same footing. The primitive churches, in the times of the apostles, first gave their own selves to the Lord, and to one another also, by the will of God, engaging to do whatever in them was to promote each other's edification and the glory of God; a man may propose himself to be a member of a church, but it is at the option of the church whether they will receive him; so Saul

assayed to join himself to the disciples, but they at first refund him, fearing he was not a true disciple; but when they had a testimony of him from Barnabas, and perceived that he was a partaker of the grace of God, and was sound in the faith of Christ, they admitted him; and it is but reasonable, a church should be satisfied in these points, as to the pet sons received into their communion; not only by a testimony of their becoming lives, but by giving an account of what God has done for their souls, and a reason of the hope that is in them; as well as by expressing their agreement with them in their articles of faith.

5. Something of this kind may be observed in all religious societies, from the beginning; see Gen. iv. 26. Exod. xxiv. 7. and so the gospel church was spoken of in prophecy, as what should be constituted and increased by agreement and covenant, Isa. xliv. 5. and hi. G, 7. Jer. 1. 5. All which agrees with New Testament language. And,

6. Such a mutual agreement is but reasonable; for how should *two walk together except they be agreed?* Amos iii. 3. And unless persons voluntarily give up themselves to a church and its pastor, they can exercise no power over them in a church way.

7. It is this confederacy, consent, and agreement, that is the formal cause of a church; it is this which not only distinguishes a church from the world, but from all other particular churches; so the church at Cenchrea was not the same with the church at Corinth, though but at a little distance from it. Onesimus and Epaphras were of the church at Collosse, and not of another, Col. iv. 9. 12. From all which it follows,

8. That a church of Christ is not *parochial,* or men do not become church members by habitation in a parish; for Turks and Jews may dwell in the same parish: nor is it *diocesan;* for we never read of more churches under one bishop or pastor, though there may have been, where churches were large, more bishops or pastors in one church, Phil. i. 1. nor *provincial,* for we read of churches in one province; as of the churches of Judea, and of Galatia, and of Macedonia: nor *national;* nay, so far from it, that

we not only read of more churches in a nation, but even of churches in houses, Rom. xvi. 5. 1 Cor. xvi. 19. Col. iv. 15. Philem. verse 2. nor *presbyterian;* for we never read of a church of presbyters or elders, though of elders ordained in churches; by which it appears there were churches before there were any presbyters or elders in them, Acts xiv. 23. But a particular visible gospel church is *congregational,* A church of saints thus *essentially* constituted, as to matter and form, have a power in this state to admit and reject members, as all societies have; and also to choose their own officers; which when done, they become a complete *organized* church, as to order and power.

Appendix B: "Of the formal cause of a particular church."

By John Owen

John Owen, *The True Nature of a Gospel Church*, in *The Works of John Owen,* edited by Thomas Russell (London, Richard Baynes, 1826). Vol. 20:370f.

The way or means whereby such persons as are described in the foregoing chapter may become a church, or enter into a church-state, is by *mutual confederation* or solemn agreement for the performance of all the duties which the Lord Christ hath prescribed unto his disciples in such churches, and in order to the exercise of the power wherewith they are intrusted according unto the rule of the word.

For the most part, the churches that are in the world at present know not *how they came so to be,* continuing only in that state which they have received by tradition from their fathers. Few there are who think that any act or duty of their own is required to instate them in church order and relation. And it is acknowledged that there is a difference between the continuation of a church and its first erection; yet that that continuation may be regular, it is required that its first congregating (for the church is a congregation) was so, as also that the force and efficacy of it be still continued. Wherefore the causes of that first gathering must be inquired into.

The churches mentioned in the New Testament, planted or gathered by the apostles, were particular churches, as hath been proved. These churches did consist each of them of many members; who were so members of one of them as that they were not members of another. The saints of the church of Corinth were not members of the church at Philippi. And the inquiry is, how those believers in one place and the other became to be a church, and that distinct from all others? The Scripture affirms in general that *they gave up themselves unto the Lord and unto the apostles,* who guided them in these affairs, by the will of God, 2

Cor. viii. 5; and that other believers were added unto the church, Acts ii. 47.

That it is the will and command of our Lord Jesus Christ that all his disciples should be joined in such societies, for the duties and ends of them prescribed and limited by himself, hath been proved sufficiently before. All that are discipled by the word are to be taught to do and observe all his commands, Matt, xxviil 19, 20.

This could *originally* be no otherwise done but by their own *actual, express, voluntary consent.* There are sundry things which concur as remote causes, *or pre-requisite conditions,* unto this conjunction of believers in a particular church, and without which it cannot be; such are baptism, profession of the Christian faith, convenient cohabitation, resorting to the preaching of the word in the same place: but neither any of these distinctly or separately, nor all of them in conjunction, are or can be the constitutive form of a particular church; for it is evident that they may all be, and yet no such church-state ensue. They cannot all together engage unto those duties nor communicate those powers which appertain unto this state.

Were there no other order in particular churches, no other discipline to be exercised in them, nor rule over them, no other duties, no other ends assigned unto them, but what are generally owned and practised in parochial assemblies, the preaching of the word within such a precinct of cohabitation, determined by civil authority, might constitute a church. But if a church be such a society as is intrusted in itself with sundry powers and privileges depending on sundry duties prescribed unto it; if it constitute new relations between persons that neither naturally nor morally were before so related, as marriage doth between husband and wife; if it require new mutual duties and give new mutual rights among themselves, not required of them either as unto their matter or as unto their manner before,— it is vain to imagine that this state can arise from or have any other formal cause but the joint consent and virtual confederation of those concerned unto these ends: for there is none of them can have any other foundation; they are all of them resolved into the wills of men, bringing themselves under an obligation unto them by their voluntary consent I say, unto the wills of men, as their formal cause; the supreme efficient cause of them all being the will, law, and constitution of our Lord Jesus Christ.

Thus it is in all societies, in all relations that are not merely natural (such as between parents and children, wherein the necessity of powers and mutual duties is predetermined by a superior law, even that of nature), wherein powers, privileges, and mutual duties, are established, as belonging unto that society. Nor, after its first institution, can anyone be incorporated into it, but by his own consent and engagement to observe the laws of it: nor, if the nature and duties of churches were acknowledged, could there be any contest in this matter; for the things ensuing are clear and evident:—

1. The Lord Christ, by his authority, hath appointed and *instituted this church-state,* as that there should be such churches; as we have proved before.

2. That, by his word or law, he hath *granted powers and privileges* unto this church, and prescribed duties unto all belonging unto it; wherein they can have no concernment who are not incorporated into such a church.

3. That therefore he doth *require* and *command* all his disciples to join themselves in such church-relations as we have proved, warranting them so to do by his word and command. Wherefore,—

4. This *joining of themselves,* whereon depend all their interest in church powers and privileges, all their obligation unto church duties, is a *voluntary act* of the obedience of faith unto the authority of Christ; nor can it be anything else.

5. Herein do they *give themselves unto the Lord* and to *one another,* by their officers, in a peculiar manner, according to the will of God, 2 Cor. viii. 5.

6. To "give ourselves unto the Lord,"—that is, unto the Lord Jesus Christ,—is expressly *to engage to do and observe all that he hath appointed and commanded* in the church, as that phrase everywhere signifieth in the Scripture; as also "joining ourselves unto God," which is the same.

7. This resignation of ourselves unto the will, power, and authority of Christ, with an express engagement made unto him of doing and observing all his commands, hath *the nature of a covenant on our part;* and it hath so on his, by virtue of the

promise of his especial presence annexed unto this engagement on our part, Matt, xxviii. 18-20.

8. For whereas there are three things required unto a covenant between God and man,—(1.) That it be of *God's appointment* and institution; (2.) That upon a prescription of duties there be a *solemn engagement* unto their performance on the part of men; (3.) That there be *especial promises of God* annexed thereunto, in which consists the matter of confederation, whereof mutual express restipulation is the form,—they all concur herein.

9. This covenant which we intend is not the covenant of grace absolutely considered; nor are all the duties belonging unto that covenant prescribed in it, but the principal of them, as faith, repentance, and the like, are presupposed unto it; nor hath it annexed unto it all the promises and privileges of the new covenant absolutely considered: but it is that which is prescribed as a *gospel duty in the covenant of grace,* whereunto do belong all the duties of evangelical worship, all the powers and privileges of the church, by virtue of *the especial promise* of the peculiar presence of Christ in such a church.

10. Whereas, therefore, in the constitution of a church, believers do give up themselves unto the Lord, and are bound solemnly to engage themselves *to do and observe all the things which Christ hath commanded* to be done and observed in that state, whereon he hath promised to be present with them and among them in an especial manner,—which presence of his doth interest them in all the rights, powers, and privileges of the church,—their so doing hath the nature of a divine covenant included in it; which is the formal cause of their church-state and being.

11. Besides, as we have proved before, there are many *mutual duties* required of all which join in church-societies, and powers to be exercised and submitted unto, whereunto none can be obliged without their own consent. They must give up themselves unto one another, by the will of God; that is, they must agree, consent, and engage among themselves, to observe all those mutual duties, to use all those privileges, and to exercise all those powers, which the Lord Christ hath prescribed and granted unto his church. See Jer. 1. 4, 5.

12. This completes the *confederation intended,* which is the formal cause of the church, and without which, either expressly or virtually performed, there can be no church-state.

13. Indeed, herein most men deceive themselves, and think they do not that, and that it ought to be done, and dispute against it as unlawful or unnecessary, which for the substance of it they do themselves, and would condemn themselves in their own consciences if they did it not. For unto what end do they join themselves unto parochial churches and assemblies? To what end do they require all professors of the protestant religion so to do, declaring it to be their duty by penalties annexed unto its neglect? Is it not that they might yield obedience unto Christ in their so doing? Is it not to profess that they will do and observe all whatsoever he commands them? Is it not to do it in that society, in those assemblies, whereunto they do belong? Is there not therein virtually a mutual agreement and engagement among them unto all those ends? It must be so with them who do not in all things in religion fight uncertainly, as men beating the air.

14. Now, whereas these things are, in themselves and for the substance of them, known gospel duties, which all believers are indispensably obliged unto, the *more express our engagement* is concerning them, the more do we glorify Christ in our profession, and the greater sense of our duty will abide on our consciences, and the greater encouragement be given unto the performance of mutual duties, as also the more evident will the warranty be for the exercise of church power. Yet do I not deny the being of churches unto those societies wherein these things are virtually only observed, especially in churches of some continuance, wherein there is at least an implicit consent unto the first covenant constitution.

15. The Lord Christ having instituted and appointed officers, rulers, or leaders, in his church (as we shall see in the next place), to look unto the discharge of all church-duties among the members of it, to administer and dispense all its privileges, and to exercise all its authority, *the consent and engagement insisted on* is expressly required unto the constitution of this order and the preservation of it; for without this no believer can be brought into that relation unto another as his pastor, guide, overseer, ruler, unto the ends mentioned, wherein he must be

subject unto him, [and] partake of all ordinances of divine worship administered by him with authority, in obedience unto the will of Christ "They gave their own selves to us," saith the apostle, "by the will of God."

16. Wherefore *the formal cause of a church* consisteth in an obediential act of believers, in such numbers as may be useful unto the ends of church-edification, jointly giving up themselves unto the Lord Jesus Christ, to do and observe all his commands, resting on the promise of his especial presence thereon, giving and communicating, by his law, all the rights, powers, and privileges of his church unto them; and in a mutual agreement among themselves jointly to perform all the duties required of them in that state, with an especial subjection unto the spiritual authority of rules and rulers appointed by Christ in that state.

17. There is nothing herein which any man who hath a conscientious sense of his duty, in *a professed subjection unto the gospel,* can question, for the substance of it, whether it be according to the mind of Christ or no; and whereas the nature and essential properties of a divine covenant are contained in it, as such it is a foundation of any church-state.

18. Thus under the Old Testament, when God would take the posterity of Abraham into a *new, peculiar church-state,* he did it by a *solemn covenant.* Herein, as he prescribed all the duties of his worship to them, and made them many blessed promises of his presence, with powers and privileges innumerable, so the people solemnly covenanted and engaged with him that they would do and observe all that he had commanded them; whereby they coalesced into that church-state which abode unto the time of reformation. This covenant is at large declared, Exod. xxiv.: for the covenant which God made there with the people, and they with him, was not the covenant of grace under a legal dispensation, for that was established unto the seed of Abraham four hundred years before, in the promise with the seal of circumcision; nor was it the covenant of works under a gospel dispensation, for God never renewed that covenant under any consideration whatever; but it was a peculiar covenant which God then made with them, and had not made with their fathers, Deut v. 2, 3, whereby they were raised and erected into a church-state, wherein they were intrusted with all the privileges and

enjoined all the duties which God had annexed thereunto. This covenant was the sole formal cause of their church-state, which they are charged so often to have broken, and which they so often solemnly renewed unto God.

19. This was that covenant which was to be *abolished,* whereon the church-state that was built thereon was utterly taken away; for hereon the Hebrews ceased to be the peculiar church of God, because the covenant whereby they were made so was abolished and taken away, as the apostle disputes at large, Heb. vii.-ix. The covenant of grace in the promise will still continue unto the true seed of Abraham, Acts ii. 38, 39; but the church-covenant was utterly taken away.

20. Upon the removal, therefore, of this covenant, and the church-state founded thereon, all duties of worship and church-privileges were also taken away (the things substituted in their room being totally of another kind). But the covenant of grace, as made with Abraham, being continued and transferred unto the gospel worshippers, *the sign or token of it* given unto him is changed, and another substituted in the room thereof. But whereas the privileges of this church-covenant were in themselves carnal only, and no way spiritual but as they were typical, and the duties prescribed in it were burdensome, yea, a yoke intolerable, the apostle declares in the same place that the new church-state, whereinto we are called by the gospel, hath no duties belonging unto it but such as are spiritual and easy, but withal hath such holy and eminent privileges as the church could no way enjoy by virtue of the first church-covenant, nor could believers be made partakers of them before that covenant was abolished. Wherefore,—

21. The same way for the erection of a church-state for the participation of the more excellent privileges of the gospel, and performance of the duties of it, for the substance of it, must still be continued; for the constitution of such a society as a church is, intrusted with powers and privileges by a covenant or mutual consent, with an engagement unto the performance of the duties belonging unto it, hath its foundation in the light of nature, so far as it hath any thing in common with other voluntary relations and societies, was instituted by God himself as the way and means of erecting the church-state of the Old Testament, and

consisteth in the performance of such duties as are expressly required of all believers.

www.ingramcontent.com/pod-product-compliance
Ingram Content Group UK Ltd.
Pitfield, Milton Keynes, MK11 3LW, UK
UKHW041914190726
13854UKWH00003B/1252